Dedication

This book is dedicated to the memory of Arnold McLay, undoubtedly one of the world's most brilliant and dedicated collectors of ornithological dejecta.

Arnold passed away in August 1986 while attempting to bring to our headquarters a rare triple splay of the Wryneck (*Jynx torquilla*), which he had managed to collect on his windscreen, some two hundred miles away in Dunbar. Unfortunately, the splay almost completely obscured his vision and in order to see properly, Arnold was forced to drive with his head protruding from the driver's window. Tragically, he was only five miles from his destination when the combined effects of exhaustion and excitement caused him to misjudge the proximity of an oncoming truck and trailer.

His decapitation, however, was not in vain. Arnold's windscreen and its remarkable splay miraculously survived the collision. It is, thankfully, preserved to this very day in the executive boardroom of the Birmingham Ornithological Dejecta Society.

In keeping with Arnold McLay's unswerving devotion to the preservation and study of splays, a commemorative plaque underneath the windscreen simply reads:

"The Last Great Splay
of the Late Arnold McLay"

Those words, that windscreen, are an inspiration to us all.

A constellation of Hairy Woodpecker *Picodes villosus* splays, The Bartle Collection.

WHAT BIRD DID THAT?

The comprehensive field guide to the ornithological dejecta of Great Britain and Europe

PETER HANSARD/BURTON SILVER

GRUB STREET • LONDON

Published by Grub Street
The Basement, 10 Chivalry Road
London SWII IHT

Originated and devised by Peter Hansard and Burton Silver

Book design and production by Trevor Plaisted, Wellington

Typeset by Megbyte Graphics, Wellington

Cover photograph by Annelies Van Der Poel

Photographs © 1991 Burton Silver

Compiled by Silverculture Press
487 Karaka Bay Road, Wellington 3, New Zealand

British Library Cataloguing in Publication Data

Hansard, Peter
    What bird did that? : the comprehensive field guide to the ornithological
    dejecta of Great Britain and Europe.
    I. Title II. Silver, Burton
    598.294

    ISBN 0948817496

Printed and bound in Hong Kong.

1 2 3 4 5 — 95 94 93 92 91

"I have always believed that birds do it quite without malice, indeed almost unconsciously, and certainly without any idea of the result. Were I to think otherwise, I would probably find it necessary to worship them. As it is I feel only a slight envy. Owls however, are quite a different matter."

Coots Na Hoot
Sir David McGill

Foreword

The noise of a bird dropping hitting a windscreen at fifty miles an hour is usually soft, muted, almost ethereal. But this one sounded like a rifle-shot. We all jumped, shaken from our silent reveries first by the sharp crack and then by the marvel of colours and textures that spread slowly upwards before us.

With skill born of great experience and dedication, the driver gradually, almost imperceptibly, slowed the car, so that now the fluids, previously held up as a bright quivering mass by the pressure of air, began to relax and glide gently downwards, spreading hues of green, crimson, white and gold in a myriad of vivid tentacles. When we finally stopped half a mile further on, at least a third of the windscreen was covered with a most magnificent splay.

There are times in one's life which are visually memorable, and other times which are intellectually memorable, but seldom, except in the greatest of films and theatre, are they ever perfectly combined. Yet this was to be such a time, for I was privileged to be sitting with Peter Hansard and Burton Silver, the world's leading experts in ornithological dejecta, while on a trip in the USA. And just inches away on the windscreen, was one of the freshest, rarest and most beautiful of all splays.

It was Burton who broke the silence. *"Gallinula chloropus? Porphyrula martinica?"* he suggested tentatively.

"Yes, I can follow your thinking on that. Look, hardly any loss of opacity, greenish-brown and virtually no envelope. But we were doing at least fifty miles an hour and a gallinule splay would have strung itself out a bit more, don't you think?"

"Maybe, but if you're talking *Anas* as I think you are, then it's rather smaller than one would expect from a mallard and anyway, how do you explain this crimson tinge here?"

"Quite possibly marsh berries — I know it's a bit late for them but it is consistent with colour and see here, this seems to be a seed casing."

"Hmm, could be insectivorous. Exoskeletal maybe. I still think a small coot or a gallinule, and perhaps a meal of marshberries swallowed whole with a small pebble. Or what about something like *Charadrius vociferus* feeding on contaminated earthworms? A piece of shell would account for the noise and a diseased soil animal would be consistent with this colour."

This fascinating discussion continued for at least fifteen minutes before they eventually agreed, by a logical process of elimination, on the Blue-winged Teal, *(Anas discors)*, with a displaced gizzard stone. Naturally, it was crucial to record this very rare splay, but they were out of film and it meant a further ten miles drive to the next town before they could load up, take some shots and then carefully scrape it off for later analysis. They drove the ten miles in great excitement and were able to purchase film from a petrol station.

We were all standing round the open boot watching Peter load the camera when it happened. A forecourt attendant casually strolled over and simply cleaned the splay right off with one of those rubber window cleaners before anyone realised what he was doing.

Now I have to say, most people would have gone berserk, screamed and yelled, threatened legal action for tampering with private property, or whatever. But not these two. No, they've just had their most significant find in years destroyed, the Dead Sea Scrolls of ornithological dejecta wiped out - and what did they do? They very calmly took that young man aside and patiently explained to him what it was he had just done. He sat and listened and like me, he became enthralled. When we drove off two hours later, he was a changed man.

Peter Hansard and Burton Silver have dedicated the last three years to the compilation of this comprehensive field guide, pooling their vast experience and knowledge so that many more of us may have the chance to become captivated by the nuances of the splay and gain a greater understanding of our feathered friends. It is a tribute to their devotion and vision that the aforementioned forecourt attendant is now president of the National Ornithological Dejecta Society and boasts a personal collection of over three thousand splays, including two of the Blue-winged Teal.

Dr Peter Twite

Contents

SPLAY TOPOGRAPHY

A knowledge of the different parts of each splay is
essential to fully describe and understand the variations in
ornithological dejecta. The diagrams below show all the
main areas of a splay as well as the main types of splay
that the collector can expect to find.
(See also Glossary of Terms.)

Sub-nucleus
Nucleus
Solids
Envelope
Outer envelope
Inner envelope
Lobe
Detached lobe
Extended lobe
Sub-nuclear particles

Splerd

*Large. Envelope covers greater
area than the nucleus which
may be almost non-existent.
Little distinction between
outer and inner envelopes.*

Sklop

*Small. Clearly defined
envelope and nucleus of
roughly equal proportions. No
tendency to lobe. Usually
taken at low speeds or results
from short drop height.*

Splood

*Varies in size. Typified by a
single extended lobe which
may contain sub-nuclear
particles and occasionally
solids.*

Schplutz

*Varies in size with multiple
extended lobes. The lower
ones may contain sub-nuclear
particles and the occasional
solid.*

Schplerter

*Large. Multiple extended and
detached lobes. Usually taken
at high speeds or results from
extended drop height. Often
has disintegrated nucleus.*

Preface

There has long been a need, not only among the motoring public, but also with an ever increasing number of bird watchers in this country, for a compact pictorial guide to the identification of ornithological dejecta. It is hoped that this book will go some way towards meeting that need and spawn other guides of a similar nature in the future.

Actual colour photographs and paintings of splays play a vital part in this work and we were indeed fortunate as authors that the many birdsplay collectors who sent in their specimens for analysis (usually presented on good quality plastic kitchen wrap), were prepared to allow us to record their most typical and significant dejecta for inclusion in this guide.

The splays chosen for this book represent a broad cross-section of avian species found throughout the region. Not all of course, are common roadside splayers; birds of general interest and one or two rarer species have been included for enlightenment, and we hope, inspiration. Batsplay is briefly discussed (to prevent confusion over nocturnal emissions) and the growing popularity of the splay as art also warrants a section. Flight silhouettes are the preferred pictorial reference; field experience indicates that such a brief and fleeting impression is usually all that can be managed prior to, or just after, splay creation.

With the growth of environmental concern in recent times, the collection and study of splays has taken on a new urgency, as its potential to provide fresh insights into the state of our habitat becomes more widely understood. In the same way that a doctor is able to gain valuable information by examining his patients' stools, so we hope this book will enable you, the reader to become more aware that splays can help us to determine, not only the health of the bird, but also the health of our environment. To this end, our guide does not concern itself with overly-specialised or detailed analysis of splays, but rather aims to provide the public with information on collection, and a simple method of identification. It is our sincere hope that everyday road users will now feel encouraged to mail samples to the National Ornithological Dejecta Society, particularly when noting interesting variations from the norm.

We are aware there are those who claim an ability to read more into bird splays, and have followed with interest a growing trend to use them to try and predict future events. However, recent claims that the general collapse of communism, and the Gulf crisis, were accurately foretold by an analysis of Greylag Goose droppings over Greenland, are not well supported.

Peter Hansard, Burton Silver
Berkeley, Calif. 1991

Introduction

While the collection of splays only became really popular with the growth of the environmental movement of the seventies, the study of avian dejecta is, nevertheless, a discipline embracing a long and rich historical tradition.

In Roman times, divination included not only the study of bird's flight patterns as a means of determining the future, but splays too, were carefully considered for their prophetic significance.

A green splay on the back of the hand was a sign of future wealth. A red splay foretold illness affecting that part of the body which had been struck. Yellow splays were seen as a sign of great success, while purple splays were the unwelcome heralds of defeat in battle.

The ancient Greeks believed that dejecta striking prospective marriage partners simultaneously, was most propitious. Indeed this sign was seen as doubly significant when the dark solids within the splay fell on the male, and the white watery parts on the female. Remnants of this belief are, of course, echoed today in the form of wedding attire; the groom is traditionally clad in black, while the bride wears white.

However it was in China, that the relationship between a bird's dietary intake and the consistency and colour of the splay was first established. The price of a caged bird was determined not only by the healthy bloom and rich colouring of its feathers, but also by the beauty and tone of its droppings. It was the fabled Mong Kok Chinese who discovered that feeding robins a diet of agapanthus seeds, tung oil and clit beetles, produced splays with a nucleus of an unusually deep turquoise, and an outer envelope which dried to a vivid blue at the extremities. The bird-sellers of Yung Shue Wan on the other hand, were famous for the scarlet and gold droppings of their nightingales, said to have been obtained by the use of a secret diet which may have included grape skins and tumeric. Deeply impressed at seeing these in presentation form, Marco Polo wrote, "bird jewels of red and gold most handsomely adorn their collars and and their cuffs."

But more importantly, it is Captain Xavier Cremment, personal communications officer to Napoleon at the time of the battles of Ulm and Austerlitz (1805), who must be credited with the pioneering research on the relationship between avian dejecta and disease. It was Cremment who first observed that the more exhausted a message-carrying pigeon became, the greener its droppings tended to be. This was a crucial factor when selecting birds to carry important orders from Napoleon to his commanders at the front line. In an eloquent demonstration now legendary among splay collectors, Captain Cremment graphically described his discoveries

Postage stamps depicting the splays of two threatened species.

while dining at the Palace of Versailles. Using cream, oysters and creme de menthe, (some accounts claim horseradish sauce and chartreuse), the resourceful captain made twenty different little splays on dark blue dinner plates bearing the gilded Napoleonic Crest. By this method, he was able to explain the gist of his findings in considerable detail.It is said that Napoleon, who had a weak stomach, never ate another oyster. However, that great culinary delicacy, pigeonneau á la sauce verte aux huîtres, (pigeon in green oyster sauce), undoubtedly owes its existence to this historic evening in the year of 1806.

In our own century, interest in avian dejecta has grown rapidly with the use of the automobile and the proliferation of roads that now reach even the most isolated habitats. There are seventeen Ornithological Dejecta Societies in the USA and over thirty in Britain. Canada has twelve Avian Splay Leagues and there are other groups in France, Italy, Australia and New Zealand.

It is a little known fact, that the New Zealand Post Office led the world in 1988, when it issued postage stamps depicting the splays of two threatened species, the North Island Kaka and the Blue Duck. The stamps were intended to help drivers identify these splays so that should they be seen on windscreens, they might then be reported to the Department of Conservation particularly if sighted in previously unrecorded habitats. The scheme proved successful; three new colonies of kaka were placed under protection in the first six months.

Similarly, a major Irish breakfast cereal company now plans the inclusion of picture-cards, depicting splays of that country's most endangered birds, in all family-packs of bran flakes.

With projects such as these already under way, and with the fast-growing acceptance of ornithological dejecta as art, it seems certain that we are about to witness a worldwide explosion of interest in the collection and study of splays.

Collection

There are over 8,350 species of flying birds and for each of them there are something like 600 possible dietary combinations. Even when ignoring factors such as seasonal fluctuations, new synthetic foods or insecticides - all of which cause excremental variations - a total of 5,000,000 quite distinctive types of birdsplay may now be collected on windscreens around the world at any one time.

Our windscreens are in fact, extremely efficient collecting nets. At just 60 MPH the average windscreen sweeps a volume of air equal to 594 cu. ft. per second. On a 60 mile journey, that's the same as spreading a net of some 396,817 sq. ft. Or, to put it another way, 100 hours of driving equates with a gigantic windscreen nearly 1.5 square miles in area, held aloft for one sixteenth of a second. With such an effective gathering device positioned in front of our eyes, it is easy to see why the growing store of fascinating information about dejecta has led to splay collection becoming a major global pastime.

The two most important factors in the capture and preservation of splays are: a collection surface enabling the splay to be easily removed, and proper observance of correct drying times so that the specimen remains intact. Most splay enthusiasts prepare the surface of their windscreen by first wiping it down with a damp cloth. A sheet of good quality clear plastic film

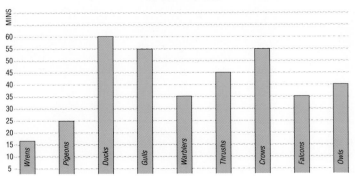

* SPLAY DRYING TIMES

SDT* FACTORS ASSUMING AN AVERAGE TEMP. OF 70F (25°C), SUMMER AND LIGHT WINDS and an average speed of 50kph or 30mph. Add 10 minutes for every 10kph or 6mph slower. Subtract 10 minutes for every 10kph or 6mph faster.

of the clingy type is then laid over the glass. Provided there is some moisture underneath, the film will remain bubble free and sit firmly in place without the need for additional fixing. Once a splay has formed on the surface, it can be easily removed with the specimen *in situ*.

Splays that strike uncovered windscreens may be loosened with a clear high-grade oil such as oleander or witch-hazel. They can then be carefully removed with a flexible blade. However, this should not be attempted until sufficient drying time has allowed the formation of a binding crust or skak (see glossary). The skak should cover the entire surface of the splay. It is also important to check that the skak is of sufficient consistency to firmly hold larger nucleic particles such as insect debris, seeds, etc. As most drying is achieved by driving which creates an air-flow over the specimen, it is necessary to be constantly alert to the danger of losing these more wind-prone pieces and thus significantly lowering the value of the splay.

Drop-height, vehicle speed, wind velocity and rain considerably affect drying time. A large, dense, fully-packed and moist splay dropped from a relatively low altitude and striking the windscreen of a stationary vehicle will, in the normal course of events, take several hours to dry. Conversely, small splays with a large drop-height will flatten and spread over the windscreen of a speeding automobile in much thinner layers. But the thinner the splay, the more likely it is to dry quickly and become brittle; your own judgement will best determine the course of action to be followed. Disintegration due to brittleness can often be prevented; a fine mist spray adaptor fitted to the windscreen washers, will prove effective. Alternatively, the car may be parked in the shade for several hours. Some collectors keep a small, damp, lightweight cloth handy and gently tape it over the splay when driving in direct sunlight.

In cold conditions, considerably increased drying times can lead to unnatural wind distortion and general splay disfigurement. The vehicle should be driven at low speeds until such time as a good skak is gradually formed. When this has been accomplished, higher speeds will then encourage drying without danger to the integrity of the splay. An S.D.T. chart has been included to indicate the drying times necessary to achieve maximum cohesion and structural strength in most splay categories. Natural fresh air remains the preferred drying method, while use of a hair-dryer is always to be avoided as it can easily alter the natural spread and texture of specimens.

The various techniques and methods of preparing and mounting splays for exhibition are too numerous and complex to be dealt with here. There are however, many excellent texts devoted to all aspects of this subject and several are listed in our bibliography.

Gavia stellata

Red-throated Diver

Description: Often of a 'tweedy' texture and colour suggesting a 'hint of the Highlands'. The malty solids are encased in a lacey envelope. So-called 'tartan splays reputedly depend upon localised tarn or loch pH factors.

Food: Aquatic animals, fish, aquatic plant matter.

Distribution: Northern parts of Ireland, Scotland and across to Scandinavia.

Collection: This is something of a rarity and would be the pride and joy of any serious student's collection. Admittedly, examples of this splay are difficult to obtain, but many northern roads do run alongside bays and lochs; simply pray that patience may be rewarded. A dual splay from this species has never been recorded.

This specimen: Near Bridge of Walls, Gruting Voe, A971, Shetlands. April 5th 1987. Fine. Light N winds, 1.30pm. Stationary vehicle.

Ardea cinerea

Grey Heron

Description: A large splay of a generous nature. Wet, fluid and impressive. It is mainly envelopic in that the core nucleus of gritty solids is thinly integrated with the whole. Low flying birds will produce more heavily impastoed dejecta.

Food: Amphibians, fish.

Distribution: Common throughout the region.

Collection: Roads skirting rivers, canals, marshes and ponds are ideal. Low speeds will produce specimens well worth collection, while higher speeds can produce spectacular results for those wishing for greater ostentation.

This Specimen:Blubberhouses near Fewston Reservoir, A59, North Yorkshire. March 16th. 1990. Showery. Light NE winds. 10MPH.

Cygnus olor

Mute Swan

Description: A graceful, semi-solid dejecta comprised almost entirely of nucleic matter (digested vegetable fibres). Splay envelopes are minimal and, in some specimens, are missing altogether. Duck-like, but bigger.

Food: Mostly aquatic plant-life, grains, occasional water insects.

Distribution: Seen on rivers, marshes and ponds throughout the region.

Collection: Prudent collectors will be aware that high speed swan splays, though spectacular, may result in windscreen coverage of an opacity and spread likely to affect road safety. Road-speeds therefore, should always be governed by circumstance.

This specimen: At Pett Level, Winchelsea Beach, East Sussex. May 16th 1988. Overcast. Calm. 10.30 am. 45 MPH.

Branta canadensis

Canada Goose

Description: Copious and sticky, very typical goose dejecta. Little envelope, mostly a greenish solid nucleus the texture of thick glue. When fresh, the powerful 'spinach soup' odour is characteristic.

Food: Vegetable matter, grains, aquatic plants, and small marine animals.

Distribution: North American species well established throughout the region.

Collection: Vigorous horn-honking may alert feeding birds, causing them to rise in startled flight by the roadside. In this situation, there is a possibility of obtaining multiple splays. Open ground or marshy expanses seem to be the preferred habitat.

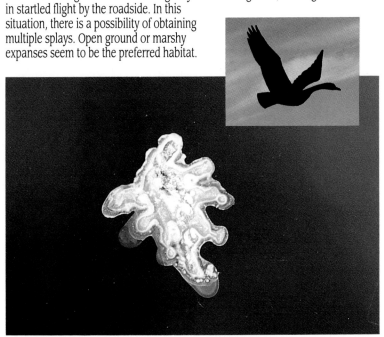

This Specimen:Near Arundel, West Sussex. May 17th 1988.
Fine, Light NE winds. 3.30pm. 32MPH.

Anas platyrhynchos

Mallard

Description: A fine cohesive splay, moist and full with little envelopic spread. Most typically, a solid, creamy grey-green dejecta displaying the satisfying texture of oil paint freshly squeezed from the tube.

Food: Aquatic plants of all descriptions, grains, water insects, small molluscs.

Distribution: Common. In abundant numbers on most lakes and marshes.

Collection: Splays are relatively common and best collected at slow speeds, on roads adjacent to inland waterways. Dual splays are often taken in the mating season and provide an excellent opportunity for comparative study.

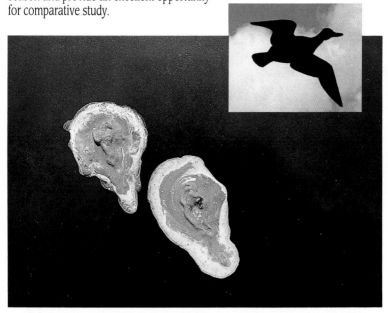

This specimen: Alongside village pond, Biddistone, Wiltshire, November 11th 1990. Overcast, light SE winds. 2.30pm. 35 MPH.

Buteo buteo

Buzzard

Description: A splay which always shows a gratifying response to drop-height. The limey envelope has the consistency of paste. The nucleus will be varied depending on diet and can show as a dark syrupy brown diluting down to light ochres and greens. The splay most popularly collected is a typically vigorous white splash.

Food: Birds and rodents.

Distribution: Scotland, N England, Wales, SW England and most of Europe. Wooded areas in general.

Collection: With the exception of the ubiquitous kestrel, raptor splays are not common and offer a degree of challenge to the enthusiast. Moderate speeds are recommended as the splay is most perfect in schplutz form.

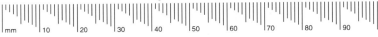

This Specimen: Near the Roman Signal Station, B8062, Strathern. December 22nd 1988. Overcast. Light N winds. 3pm. 35MPH.

Falco peregrinus

Peregrine Falcon

Description: Like all falcons, has a steady splay forming a series of long sploodish threads (falcon droppings simply fall from the cloaca - whereas hawks eject their dejecta in powerful squirts). Wet and limey. Variation limited but look for green sub-nucleic 'freckles' during breeding season.

Food: Small birds.

Distribution: Widespread throughout the region, but rare.

Collection: Popularly known as the duck hawk, the peregrine's splay is usually seen near nesting sites or roosts; windscreen examples have a rarity value and are much prized by the collector. Coastal, farmland and high altitude areas are recommended.

This specimen: Near Bont Dolgadfan, B4518, Powys. October 3rd 1989. Rain. NW winds. 10.50 am. 45MPH.

Falco tinnunculus

Kestrel

Description: A medium-small splay. Dejecta ejected on occasions from a height of one hundred feet or more. The copious creamy envelope contains a handsome brown nucleus, giving ample evidence of the insectivorous diet. Because of drop-height, often thinly spread in a sunburst pattern.

Food: Mostly insectivorous.

Distribution: Widespread. Commonly seen by roadsides.

Collection: Birds criss-crossing motorways as they work one verge and then the other, offer the best opportunity for collection. Motorway speeds however, tend to disperse solids in an unnatural manner.

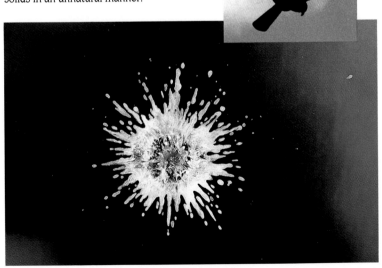

This specimen: Route de Marseille 26200, Montelimar. September 5th 1990. Fine, hot and calm. 11.25am. 30 MPH

Perdix perdix
Partridge

Description: A full-bodied but surprisingly small sklop, tacky to the touch. Richly textured and tightly packed within its envelopic outer. Colourful solids will reward serious study as seasonal food changes make for vivid splay-palette contrasts.

Food: Mostly vegetable. Grains, berries, small ground insects.

Distribution: Throughout the British Isles and Europe.

Collection: Slow speeds on country lanes bring the best results. Quarry flies speedily (and at a low height). Splays intended for exhibition should resemble natural ground droppings as closely as possible. Horn-blasting may help to flush quarry.

This specimen: By High Halden, A28, Kent. July 20th 1986.
Bright, Light W winds. 11.40 am. 30 MPH.

Phasianus colchicus

Pheasant

Description: Generous and wet with a tendency to splood. A viscous nucleus tends to spread its large fruity solids broadly within the envelope. Warm tonings in autumn are indicative of the availability of nuts, berries, etc.

Food: Omnivorous: seeds, berries, leatherjackets, even voles.

Distribution: Introduced from Asia in medieval times, now widespread and common throughout region.

Collection: Flies rapidly and low over roads, from field to field. Most country lanes are fertile areas for collection, especially during the shooting season when splays tend to be somewhat loose and more frequent. Drop-height will not affect splay but high speeds are best avoided. Sounding the horn is effective.

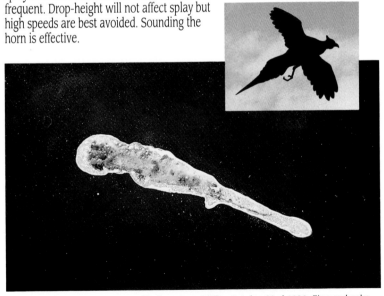

This specimen: A363, near Bradford-on-Avon, Wilts. October 23rd 1990. Fine and calm. 1pm. 40 MPH.

Fulica atra

Coot

Description: Fluid, oily, stringy. A weak envelope surrounds the loose, greenish core. This splay is normally a schplerter with a multiplicity of detached lobes. In the finest examples, these form even more extended lobular patterns (splays within splays).

Food: Aquatic plant and insects.

Distribution: Commonly seen in parks, rivers, flooded gravel pits, marshland, etc. throughout region.

Collection: Drop-height will vary and splay viability cannot always be successfully maintained at high road speeds. Experimentation will soon indicate which textures and patterns best suit your requirements. As for getting them to rise - as a splayman always says, 'it pays to toot a coot.'

This specimen: Church Street by River Avon, Bradford-on-Avon, Wilts. November 2nd 1986. Overcast. Brisk S winds. 2.30pm. 25 MPH.

Vanellus vanellus

Lapwing

Description: Wet and earthy upon release but rapidly drying to a brittle 'pie crust' consistency. Envelope and nucleus often merge on impact. The schplutz form is typical. Look for sandy soil fragmentation within the nucleus and intricate starburst patterns in the outer envelope.

Food: Pasture insects, worms, etc.

Distribution: Widespread. Easily the most common inland plover.

Collection: Simply drive alongside arable land. Lapwings generally provide splays from a drop-height anywhere up to 70 feet. 'Wormy' examples are much prized if fresh and pink. Weather clearing after rain should provide ideal conditions for collection. Speeds are best kept moderate to preserve form and texture.

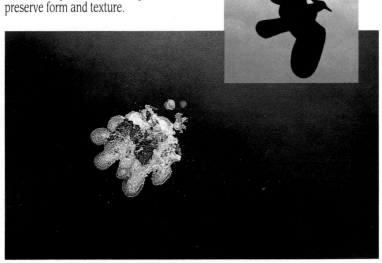

This specimen: Near Pett Level, Winchelsea Beach, E. Sussex. May 16th 1988.
Overcast. Light N winds. 2.30pm. 35 MPH.

Calidris canutus

Knot

Description: Pert and perky. A fairly opaque and reasonably solid dejecta with little envelope and, as is the case with most ducks, a thick sticky texture, with those much prized yellow and purple tints embellishing the overall greenish-grey hue.

Food: Small marine animals, etc.

Distribution: Winters on the coasts of Britain, France, Spain, N Africa.

Collection: You will need to find roads close to estuaries and bays. Knots rise and wheel in flocks numbering hundreds of thousands. Multiple strikes (very desirable) are often obtained in the much-favoured 'polka' dot pattern which may consist of as many as forty individual splays.

This specimen: Estuary (Great Eau) near Saltfleet, off A1031, Lincolnshire. February 12th 1986. Showery, Brisk NE winds. 2.45pm. 45 MPH.

```
mm    10    20    30    40    50    60    70    80    90
```

Scolopax rusticola

Woodcock

Description: Earthy and fibrous nucleus merging with a dull and sombre envelopic outer. A splay most generally of the schplutz type. However, barely detached lobes sometimes qualify it as a conservative form of schplerter.

Food: Insects, worms, small soil animals.

Distribution: Resident throughout Britain and France.

Collection: Try roads near forests or heathlands. The usually solitary male encircles his territory at dawn and again at dusk. Once obtained, this splay usually remains viable over a wide range of driving conditions.

This specimen: Ashdown Forest, E. Sussex. October 7th 1987. Fair, light NW winds. 2.15pm. 50 MPH.

Larus argentatus

Herring Gull

Description: A large white limeaceous splay of surprising density and volume. The very large nucleus varies in colour and texture according to diet, and will range from a dramatic dark and gritty solid to a paste or gruel featuring delicate shades of cream.

Food: Indiscriminate scavenger. Fish, shellfish, crabs, mice, eggs, insects, bread.

Distribution: The most common large gull. Widespread throughout most of the region.

Collection: Herring gull splays are readily collected in the parking lots of fast food outlets and on roads surrounding rubbish tips. At the seashore, splaying can be encouraged by tossing bread into the air in the vicinity of the vehicle. Multiple splays are common.

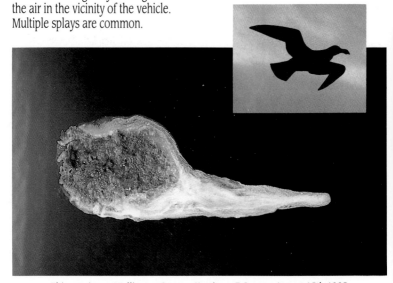

This specimen: Wellington Square, Hastings, E Sussex. August 15th 1985. Overcast. E winds off the sea. 3.30pm. Stationary vehicle.

Larus ridibundus

Black-headed Gull

Description: A large splay from a medium-sized (14-15", 35-38cms) bird. White and limey with entertaining oily solids spread throughout. Omnivorous diet allows for variable splay colours and textures.

Food: Crabs, fish scraps, aquatic animals, etc.

Distribution: Widespread. Tends to drift inland during winter.

Collection: Try coastal roads for the true 'fishy' splays of summer; rubbish dumps or playing fields for darker, 'gloomier' winter splays. Average speeds will produce 'frilled' envelope effect - experiment with other forms of driving to produce controlled spread. Ploughed fields and animals killed on the road attract this species.

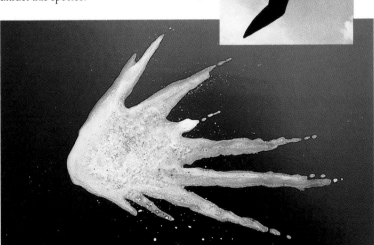

This specimen: South Undercliff, near The Saltings, Rye. E. Sussex. November 22nd 1985. Light showers. Calm. 1.25pm. 38 MPH.

Sterna hirundo

Common Tern

Description: A splood. Summery, light, precise, as neat as the bird itself. Splays are medium-sized, white, with a sooty nucleic core. Look for occasional green pigmentation of sub-nucleic solids in the breeding season.

Food: Small fish.

Distribution: A common breeding visitor during summer months. Widespread. Seen near fresh water inland.

Collection: Roads near beachfronts, estuaries, lakesides, or island coastlines in summer. All offer the collector opportunities for satisfying splays. Responds dramatically to high speed impacts.

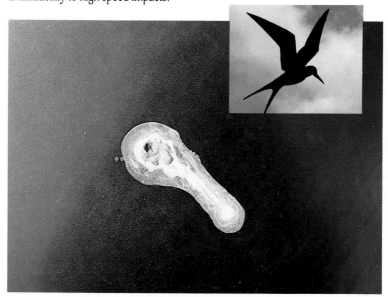

*This specimen: Avonmouth, near Bristol. June 22nd 1990. Fair.
Light N winds. 2.20 pm. 45 MPH.*

Columba palumbus

Woodpigeon

Description: A typical splutz. Soft and fruity, loose and wet. Mainly envelopic with clear distinctions between outer and inner envelopes. Well defined nucleus often contains large undigested solids.

Food: Berries, seeds, crop foods, leafy vegetable matter.

Distribution: A widespread resident throughout Britain and Europe.

Collection: Easily obtained whilst driving by tree-lined avenues or parks in cities, by arable land or woods in the country. This soft splay will readily distort at speed. Drop-height sometimes up to 60 feet. Blowing the horn will encourage ejection of dejecta, but resulting splays often display an unacceptable fluidity.

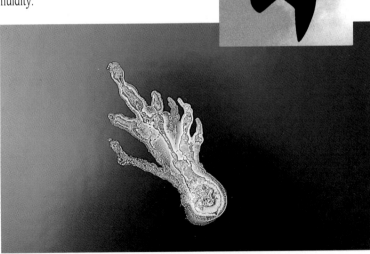

This specimen: Near Limpley Stoke, Wilts. Blustery SW gusts.
November 21st 1990. 2.45pm. 25 MPH.

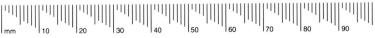

Columba livia

Feral Pigeon

Description: A generous schplutz with green, brown and occasionally yellow nuclear material, tending to be well spread within the somewhat loose envelope. Dries to a hard and brittle consistency.

Food: Grain, scraps, such left-overs as humanity may endow.

Distribution: Widespread throughout the region's cities and towns.

Collection: Street parking in any town usually brings a good result. If speed-splays only will satisfy, then driving should be kept to normal speeds. Rapid disintegration can occur if persistent showery conditions are encountered.

This specimen: Rue des Rosiers, Saint Quen. August 25th 1990.
Fine, hot and calm. 11.05 am. 15 MPH.

Cuculus canorus

Cuckoo

Description: Very runny. A long and streaky slash - a king of extended splood. Contains a nucleus of grey solids, liberally sprinkled with green and rufous flecks. Seasonal tonings have been observed.

Food: Insects of all descriptions.

Distribution: Summer migrant common across the region.

Collection: One of the real joys of early summer is the gentle 'plop' of the first cuckoo splay of the year striking a sunlit windscreen. Any leafy lane is worth investigation, but keep speeds under 25 MPH for a pleasant, naturally formed example.

This specimen: Dead Man's Lane, Rye, E.Sussex. May 15th 1987.
Fine, light breeze from NW. 12.15pm. 10 MPH.

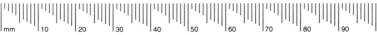

Tyto alba

Barn Owl

Description: A globular splash prone to considerable lobular extension upon impact. Fascinatingly bland as skeletal and fur remnants of prey are largely regurgitated in the form of 'pellets' (of no interest to the splayman) without passing through intestinal tract.

Food: Mainly rodents. Large insects.

Distribution: Widespread resident of the area.

Collection: Crepuscular and night driving near rural buildings, churches etc. recommended. Bird appears ghostly white in headlights. When parked at night, wind down window and try imitating this owl's call: a strangled shriek or an eerie rasping hiss.

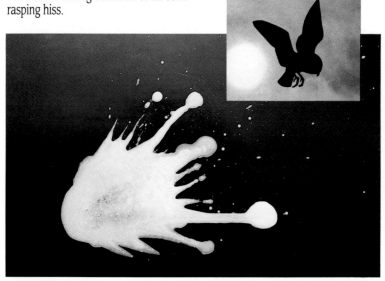

This specimen: By Beziers, Languedoc. May 14th 1985. Clear and calm. 9.45pm. 40 MPH.

Strix aluco

Tawny Owl

Description: A generous squirt of a splay. Streaky white and limey with little nucleic core differentiation (see Barn owl, ref. 'pellets'). An influx of any one particular prey species in an owl's territory may affect the overall colour and tonings of the white splay and result in a riotous splash of exuberant ivory-creams.

Food: Rodents. Small birds.

Distribution: Right across Britain and Continental Europe.

Collection: Night driving near urban parks and gardens can prove successful. To avoid excessive deformation, keep speeds very slow. Cruising the block with headlights extinguished and 'hooting' softly through your open window, will bring good results.

This specimen: By Church Square Police Building, Rye, E Sussex. July 20th 1984. Overcast. NW winds. 11.50pm. 5 MPH.

Apus apus

Swift

Description: Small, sooty, not always seen in natural rounded sklop form as drop-height is often considerable. Interesting darker solids in the nucleus unmistakably point to an insectivorous diet.

Food: Flying insects.

Distribution: Summer visitor, breeds throughout region.

Collection: Late afternoon and early evening are good times for collection as swifts will be noted busily feeding on the wing while rapidly circling church steeples, houses, treetops etc. Slow speeds are recommended.

This specimen: Near Radcliffe Camera, A4158, Oxford.
Fine and calm. June 20th 9.30pm. 12 MPH.

Alcedo atthis

Kingfisher

Description: A wet and rather oily splod of average size. The thick creamy envelope contains a weak yet subtly toned nucleus. A versatile diet allows for considerable variation in this much prized if somewhat odoriferous splay.

Food: Small fish.

Distribution: England, Wales, Continental Europe. Not resident in Scotland.

Collection: Drive quietly and slowly alongside canals, rivers etc. In winter, try marine drives near estuaries etc. although sometimes birds come into river towns during colder weather.

This specimen: On the bridge, Bradford-on-Avon, Wilts. December 20th 1990. Overcast and calm. 2.30pm. 5 MPH.

Picus viridis

Green Woodpecker

Description: A small slop of tightly packed consistency and firm rounded contours. Clearly defined inner and outer envelopes surrounding a loose nucleus. Look for exoskeletal remnants.

Food: Insects.

Distribution: England, Wales, most of Europe.

Collection: The machine-gun sound of a woodpecker drumming in wooded areas will alert you to its whereabouts. Proceed slowly, keeping engine noise low and watching for birds on tree-trunks.
Continual reversing backwards then forward will, over a period of time, help birds become accustomed to your presence.

This specimen: Snatts Road, Uckfield, E Sussex. September 3rd 1990.
Fine, light NW breeze. 12 noon. 35 MPH.

mm   10   20   30   40   50   60   70   80   90

Alauda arvensis

Skylark

Description: A small but perfectly formed splay of brownish hue, nicely accentuated by its envelopic encapsulation of frothy cream. Tiny, but pleasantly sculptural in form and always a delight to the eye. Check for expressive solids of an insectivorous nature.

Food: Mostly seeds.

Distribution: Well distributed throughout entire region.

Collection: Roads in grassy open countryside offer best splay chances. In winter and during migration when larks flock, multiple splays become a distinct possibility. Airborne song display readily identifies this species in the field.

This specimen: Near Widecombe-in-the-Moor, Devon. June 12th 1985.
Patchy skies, light breezes from the north. 6.30am. 45 MPH.

Hirundo rustica

Swallow

Description: Small, pert, sklopic if undistorted. The experienced eye will immediately detect signs of an insectivorous diet. Cream and chocolate blend harmoniously at the junction of the intermediary envelope.

Food: Insects (midges, gnats, etc.).

Distribution: Common. Summer breeding visitor across the region.

Collection: These swallows nest in all manner of man-made buildings, ceaselessly flying back and forth during daylight hours. Overhead wires offer an additional source of splays; remember, the courteous splayman will always show consideration for other motorists and adjust speeds according to the flow of traffic.

This specimen: Bohemia Road, Hastings, E Sussex. August 19th 1985.
Overcast. Rain. Calm. 12.45pm. 25 MPH.

Motacilla alba

Pied Wagtail

Description: A typical insectivorous sklop. Examples showing clean separation of inner and outer envelope (uncontaminated by gritty solids) are most prized. Nucleus is dark and mottled and often has a curled 'Mr Whippy' topping.

Food: Flying insects.

Distribution: Well represented across entire region.

Collection: Where insects abound, a pied wagtail will most likely be found on the hunt. Usually, water of some description (whether puddle or river) is not far away. Roads near fresh water and its margins are recommended. More rural in winter. Slow speeds are best to avoid distortion and maintain the curled topping of the nucleus.

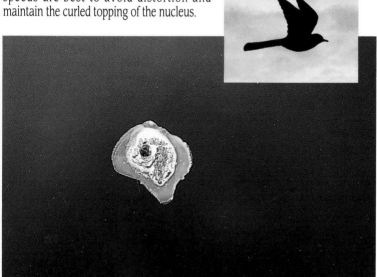

This specimen: Near Sissinghurst, Kent. July 29th 1986. Fine. S breezes. 3.20pm. 18 MPH.

Regulus regulus

Goldcrest

Description: More of a speck than a splay, but a huge asset to the collection of any serious student of ornithological dejecta. Surprisingly well formed with little or no nucleus. Magnification reveals a delicate thread-like aura. The splay collectors 'pearl'.

Food: Flies, insects (including spiders.)

Distribution: Resident across the region's woodlands. Marked preference for conifers in summer, spreading to shrubs and bushes in winter.

Collection: One of the region's most desirable splays it responds well to collection on plastic film spread over the windscreen. This allows for detailed examination under a microscope at a later time when it can be distinguished from flattened mosquito bodies which it can often resemble. Roads in woodland areas are best and a very slow speed is advisable to prevent disintegration.

This specimen: Point Hill, Rye, E Sussex. August 30th 1985.
Light S winds. 11.15am. 40 MPH.

Muscicapa striata

Spotted Flycatcher

Description: The so-called 'doily' splay. A medium-small sklop, betraying signs of an insectivorous diet. The dark and compact nucleus is nicely encircled by an envelope with the intricate patterns of a white lace doily.

Food: Mostly flies. Occasionally takes earthworms and berries, making for varietal dejecta of a rarer and highly collectable nature.

Distribution: Summer breeding visitor across region.

Collection: An unobtrusive species frequenting suburban gardens. May well be found fairly close to your garage. Reversing up and down your drive all Sunday morning is well worthwhile and may have your neighbours taking an interest.

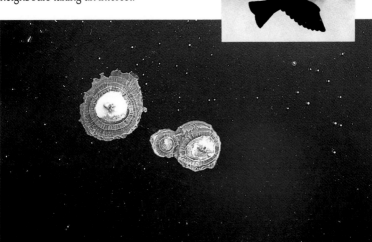

This specimen: Off B1073, near River Orwell, Ipswich, Suffolk. June 29th 1985. Light SE winds. 2.30pm. 7 MPH.

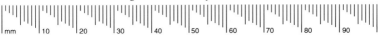

Erithacus rubecula

Robin

Description: Medium-small but extrovert in character. A fairly loose and squishy dejecta, with a tendency to splood. The thick milky-white envelope usually contains a colourful variety of partially digested solids which may become sub-nuclear.

Food: Garden insects, larvae, fruit, seeds, worms.

Distribution: Widespread. Common.

Collection: Generally a common resident of parks and gardens; suburban driving should offer plenty of opportunity. Drop-height will always be low but the loose nature of this splay would indicate lower speeds to maintain viability. Splays with berry traces matching the colour of an adult bird's breast, are considered highly desirable.

This specimen: Cathedral Close, Salisbury, Wilts. November 5th 1990.
Light drizzle. Calm. 1.45pm. 15 MPH.

Turdus merula

Blackbird

Description: An extended sklop with an attractive cloud-like appearance. Moist, loose, fragile. The nucleus lacks the ability to retain even small gritty solids, which tend to spread throughout the envelope.

Food: Insects, larvae, slugs, fruit, seeds.

Distribution: Resident, widespread and common.

Collection: Another common garden bird; suburban and city driving will suffice. A low drop-height is to be expected. A range of seasonal splays will make a handsome display. If wishing to collect locally, simply keep circling the area very slowly. (Should you arouse suspicion in the neighbourhood and the police arrive, be sure to check the windscreen of their patrol car too).

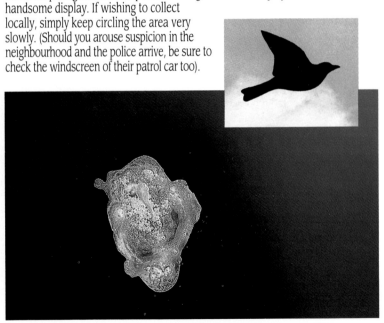

This specimen: Fuller Avenue, Royal Tunbridge Wells, June 15th. 1990.
Fine. NW winds. 10.15am. 36 MPH.

Turdus philomelos

Song Thrush

Description: A rather loosely formed schplutz. The creamy textured splay is often garnished with bright streaks and flecks (seasonal fruits and berries). Solids suggesting an invertebrate intake are invariably found floating in the nucleus.

Food: Snails, worms, insects, berries, seeds.

Distribution: Resident, widespread and common.

Collection: A thrush splay may be collected at any time of day. After rain, drive past grassy verges where birds may be seen looking for worms on the surface. Birds appear to be tamer during winter when food is harder to come by. The thrush enjoys a good feed of snails, and half a dozen of these tasty creatures moving about on the bonnet, may be just what's needed to entice *Turdus* into range.

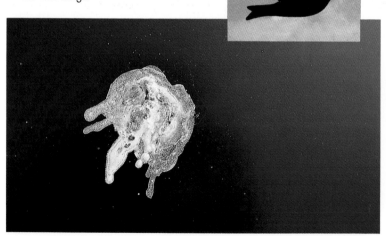

This specimen: By The Armoury, Castle St. Winchelsea. E Sussex. August 21st 1986. 3.15pm. 40 MPH.

Parus caeruleus

Blue Tit

Description: A tight little schplerter that rewards the collector with excellent examples of starbursting even from low drop-heights. Close examination may reveal evidence of an insectivorous diet.

Food: Insects (aphids, caterpillars etc.) seeds, grains, fruits.

Distribution: Widespread and common.

Collection: A tireless feeder during the busy breeding season. Flits from garden to garden during winter when food is scarce and bird feeders are lifesavers. NB: Attachment of peanut dispensers to the exterior of vehicles is something no self respecting splay-collector can possibly countenance.

This specimen: Upton St. Leonards, off M5, Gloucestershire. November 7th 1985. Overcast. NE winds. 1.00pm. 40MPH.

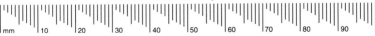

52

Fringilla coelebs
Chaffinch

Description: A small, compact, mainly envelopic splutz, which at times can be brightly coloured. Often sticky transparent residue replaces the normal secondary envelope. Check nucleus for signs of undigested seeds or insect material.

Food: Predominantly a seed-eater. Also beech-mast.

Distribution: Widespread and common resident.

Collection: Birds move through their territories on a regular basis. Use binoculars to carefully scan neighbouring gardens and establish arrival and departure times. Drop-height will be low and the small size and tight formation of this splay suits collection at almost any speed.

This specimen: La Croisette, Cannes, May 14th 1987. Rain. Calm. 1.30pm. 40 MPH.

Carduelis carduelis

Goldfinch

Description: Small, sometimes only the size of a grain of rice. The coiled, rather gaudy and squishy nucleus is delightfully encapsulated in a semi-opaque, frothy envelope.

Food: A variety of seeds. Fruits, some insects during breeding cycle.

Distribution: Resident, widespread throughout the area. Less common than formerly.

Collection: Drive past garden areas, railway embankments and wastelands when weeds are seeding etc. Expect low drop-height. This tight little sklop usually tolerates a wide variety of driving conditions.

This specimen: Near Colchester, Essex, A133. June 15th 1985. Dull. Light N breezes. 11.20am. 45 MPH.

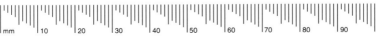

Passer domesticus

House Sparrow

Description: Small but cheekily extrovert in nature. Nucleic core is a turbulent mix of grey and brown, porridge-grey envelope prone to extravagant starburst formation.

Food: Anything going (bread etc) but mainly grains and weed seeds.

Distribution: Resident. Widespread. Common.

Collection: Bread can be used as an effective enticement. Watch for sparrows pulling at yellow crocus petals in springtime. These may add a pleasant saffron glow to an otherwise subfuscous palette.
Tried coloured pop-corn on the bonnet? Some NODS members would not approve, but it is effective.

This specimen: Avenue Albert 1er St. Jean, Cap Ferrat. May 25th 1987. 9.00am. 65 MPH.

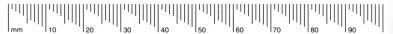

Sturnus vulgaris

Starling

Description: Med-small. A sploshy splotch of a splay. Thick white envelope with a juicy nucleus, sometimes vulgar because pretentious. Will radiate dramatically on impact to form thin, semi-opaque, often bubbly starburst showing much lobular extension. A true schplerter when speed and drop-height are favourable.

Food: Soil insects, worms, spiders, snails, slugs. Also seeds, fruits and berries in season.

Distribution: Resident. Widespread over region. Common.

Collection: One could spend a lifetime delving into the intricacies of starling splays alone. A wide range of dietary substances combined with seasonal variations make for ever-changing splay factors. If lucky enough to park under a communal roost, the splay enthusiast will be richly rewarded.

This specimen: Courbevoie, Paris. May 7th 1984. Fine and calm. 6.15pm. 38 MPH.

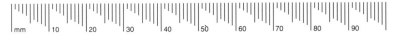

Pica pica

Magpie

Description: A medium-sized splay, generally splashing in a manner befitting such a confident and aggressive bird. White and limey envelope. A varied nucleus, usually brownish-grey but some attractive yellows or even orange tonings may be present if fruit or berries are in season.

Food: Omnivorous. Eggs and young of smaller birds, frogs, snails, insects, carrion, bread scraps.

Distribution: Widespread.

Collection: Often seen in pairs, the collector will readily spot them in towns, villages and rural areas. High speeds and a relatively high drop-height will combine to produce splays of a satisfactorily graphic nature.

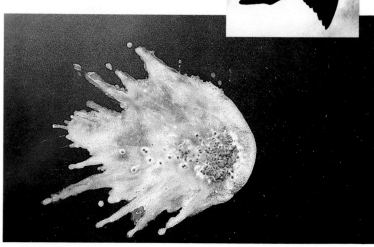

This specimen: Near Natwest car park, Trowbridge, Wilts. November 19th 1990.
Rain. Stiff W breeze. 1.20pm. 40 MPH.

Corvus frugilegus

Rook

Description: A confident medium-large splay comprised of a thin, loose, pasty outer envelope with a pronounced tendency to spread and streak. Often the nucleus is 'sludgey'. Partially digested solids enliven the otherwise graphically bland and 'whitewashed' appearance of this splay.

Food: Soil insects and their larvae. Worms, snails, grain, seeds, fruit. Occasional carrion etc.

Distribution: Resident. Widespread and common on farmland.

Collection: Those unconcerned with accurate nucleic preservation (not always an essential factor in *Corvidae* exhibits) can enjoy a liberated approach to collection. With a relatively high drop-height, a stiff head-wind and speeds of up to 80 MPH, magnificent splays of up to four feet across are entirely possible. Rain helps to achieve greater spread.

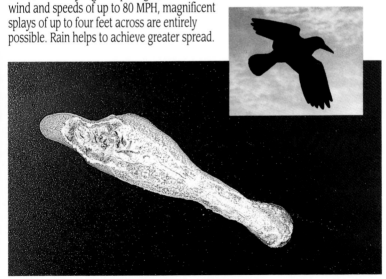

This specimen: By fields at Pett Levels, near Winchelsea Beach, E Sussex. July 1986. Fine. NE breeze. 5.30pm. 60 MPH.

mm　10　20　30　40　50　60　70　80　90

Bat Splay
A short note on the Chiroptera

Although bats are the only mammal that can actually fly, their dejecta is usually of little real significance or interest because unlike avian splays, it lacks an outer envelope and is comprised of an unpleasant and cohesive monochrome nucleus, decidedly 'mousey' in smell, and with little real potential for graphic starbursting of exhibition quality.

'Large aerial mouse-droppings' might at first seem to be an apt description, but batsplays can sometimes be remarkably fluid and sticky. No doubt slight tonal variations and a shift in faecal hue can occur, but without the contrast of a splashing white envelope, so readily and happily associated in our minds with birdsplays, there is generally little to fire, or even capture, the imagination.

An exception could perhaps be made in the case of the three species of Vampires, all of which are New World fauna. After feeding on the blood of cattle or mules, they return to their colonies and produce amazingly pungent and syrupy dejecta of a rich, streaky brown.

The flight silhouette given here, seeks to represent the typical sighting, and is included purely to help avoid confusion with bird species sometimes seen hawking for insects at dusk (swifts, swallows, martins. etc.). As a splay forming on the windscreen at night, cannot always be presumed to have come from a species of owl or some other night flying bird (gulls and migrating species often fly great distances on clear nights), it follows therefore, that occasionally, bats will be responsible.

Hopefully, by using the guidelines mentioned above (lack of envelope, 'mousey' smell, etc), such dejecta can safely be identified and destroyed forthwith.

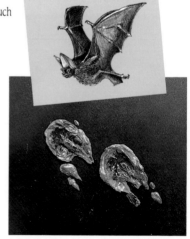

The splay of the Common Short-nosed Fruit Bat, *Cynopterus marginatus*

A dual splay of the Common Blood Sucking Vampire, *Desmodus rufus*

The Splay as Art

Interest in well-framed specimens of avian dejecta is hardly confined to those of an ornithological persuasion. In recent years, the splay has gained increasing attention within the established art community. Mounted splays both real and artificial, while admittedly still a controversial element of the art scene, are beginning to command high prices. A dual splay of the Blue Winged Teal, dated 1983, was sold recently in a leading Dallas gallery for $6000. Similar prices for top quality compositions have been obtained in London's Cork Street. This trend comes as a surprise to the many who question whether splays can truly be works of art.

There are two major schools of thought on this. On the one hand, there are those who simply see the splay as falling within the broad context of found art. This method allows that art is what an artist says it is, and that if a splay collector says his exhibit is art, then so it is. On the other hand, there are those led by David Hinds, Curator of the Department of Arts, University of Bristol, England, who see the splay as having an important place in what has become known as the Green Movement. This movement, sometimes called Behavioural Art, has strong links with abstract expressionism, and its leading exponent, Jackson Pollock, created many famous splay-like compositions curiously reminiscent of areas surrounding large communal roosts.

Abstract expressionists shunned the idea of producing purely representational images and instead, expressed themselves by the manner in which they applied paint to canvas. It could be rolled, poured, brushed, smeared, trickled or thrown. The crucial thing always, was that the feeling that lay behind the doing of the work had to be communicated within the final image. David Hinds argues that, "the mounted and framed dejecta of a bird is not excrement in the artistic sense, but rather an expressively applied image. When you look at a splay you will immediately recognise the manner in which it was cast down. In precisely the same way, you can immediately recognise how Pollock felt when he applied paint to canvas. You can sense a forceful or irritated expulsion in some dejecta, just as you might sense that certain other splays have been released gently with a feeling of quiet relief. So by viewing a splay in an artistic context, you achieve greater empathy with the bird itself...even the most insensitive people get to feel differently about a little bitty brown sparrow poop compared to the huge creamy white splash from a low flying cormorant."

Essentially, the Green Movement views the splay as a viable artistic message, one that apart from telling us what the bird in question may have been eating, allows us to get in touch with a particular bird's feelings. In the early 90's, the movement has gone even further with artists such as Busch and Rewi in Ireland, and Hillary and Holden in America, attempting a much deeper involvement with the bird by imitating its excremental method.

Application is by two rubber tubes joined together to represent the ureter or cloaca found at the posterior end of the bird's alimentary tract. Each is filled with a paint substitute for the urate (white, liquid) and faecal (dark, solid) splay components, then held high above the canvas. The artist often prefers to adopt an avian posture while meditating in a bird-like state. Some painters flap their arms and even emit chirping sounds. At the precise moment of greatest excremental empathy, the tubes are squeezed, sometimes with actual buttock pressure, and a 'splay' is formed on the canvas.

No matter how experimental an art form seems to be, no matter what medium is used or what movement or school it claims to belong to, the basic criteria that make for art always remain the same. These criteria are: structure, form, composition and integrity; without these, critics agree, no old master or modern abstract painting can be taken seriously. How then does the splay measure up to these criteria?

The splay has structure, because it is solidly based on dynamic geometric principles. It is forced by muscular spasm and intestinal dimensions into a structural whole. The splay has form too, because the interplay between dark and light tones prevents it from looking entirely flat. The texture, the wonderful chiaroscuro emanating from the interaction between envelope and nucleus, suggests technique, style and above all, visual reality.

It is in the area of composition that splays sometimes fail as art. Usually this occurs when the exhibit is mounted and framed in a way that disregards the 'Golden Rule'. This dictates an exterior proportion of any size proportionately equivalent to 13 x 8, (portrait or landscape) but insists on extra width at the bottom of the mount so that the whole is naturally pleasing to the eye. When this convention is properly observed the splay is immediately brought within the realms of true art.

Finally, integrity. We need be in no doubt in this regard; one only has to look at a splay to realise it was 'meant'.

Rewi's *'Spasm'* on show at the Natural Image Gallery in Dublin.

Acknowledgements

Planning, research, writing and photography for this guide have taken the best part of three years to complete. We are deeply indebted to the many people who have given so generously of their time and knowledge during this period.

Special thanks is gladly given to the many dedicated members of Ornithological Dejecta Societies (on both sides of the Atlantic), who so willingly assisted with the collection and photography of splays. Without their help and encouragement, this book could not have been produced.

We owe a great debt to the president of the National Ornithological Dejecta Society of America, Bob Brockie, who in the last year alone, travelled more than 6000 miles in order to determine the exact splay drying times for species included in this edition. Also Erena Rutherford and Astrid Malcolm whose splay reconstruction work has been of inestimable value. Working non-stop over a three month period, this dedicated pair successfully rebuilt the rarely obtained splay of a Common Loon, *Gavia immer*, from nearly two thousand tiny dry fragments.

We are grateful to Graham McMahon who supplied detailed information on methods of determining splay consistency prior to their transfer, and to Ashley Conland who generously shared information on swept volume, capture time and the blur factor, from his own research papers prior to publication.

We also acknowledge our debt to Dr Pat Norris, whose analysis of genuine splays found in cabinets of early taxidermy has been invaluable. And we would certainly fail in our duty if we did not express our appreciation of the outstanding collection work of Captain Nick Dryden. A typical example of the dedication he has shown over the last three years is illustrated by the removal of the wheelhouse window aboard his trawler during atrocious conditions in the Southern Ocean. The window had been struck by a six foot wide splay of a Wandering Albatross, *Diomedea exulans*, and was, remarkably, returned to harbour intact.

But our greatest single debt is to Heather Busch who devoted two years of her time, without remuneration, to extensive travel in the British Isles, Europe and North America. Photographing splays in conditions that proved extremely trying, Heather's VW van had to be shared with three dogs, two cats and a parrot. Thank you Heather, Floyd, Oddy, Sod, Lixy, Lozenge and Bigbit.

P.H. & B.S.

Glossary

APR Avian Preference Ranking. Refers to the relative likelihood of a surface being covered by a splay. The windscreen of a moving vehicle has a high APR as does the top of the head.

audibon soft sound made by avian dejecta as it strikes a windscreen and forms a splay. Audi (l) sound, bon (fr) good, literally, good sound.

avian of the bird kind.

bogor dry or semi-dry splay, broken into pieces during an attempt at removal from the original surface. A bogor may be reassembled and glued to another surface, but it always remains a bogor.

chewits dried flakes of splay which collect along the upper surface of windscreen wiper blades and give the impression that the rubber has been chewed. Chewits may also find their way into the air-intake vents below the windscreen, and create an interesting miniature snowstorm effect throughout the vehicle when the ventilation fan is first turned on.

clap-trapping use of loud clapping or horn blowing to startle birds into low flight defecation in the vicinity of a surface designed to trap the resultant splay. The use of this technique, while effective, is frowned upon by some British dejecta societies.

capture time time taken for dejecta to fall the depth of a windscreen. Depends on drop-height, depth of windscreen and speed of vehicle. Dejecta ejected at 100 feet, in the vicinity of a vehicle with a 1.5 foot high windscreen, travelling at 60 M.P.H., would have a capture time of one sixteenth of a second.

constellation group of splays with many tiny associated star-like splatter specks giving the appearance of the night sky.

dejecta excrement.

dooby incomplete or partial splay caused by dejecta breaking up prior to being formed into a splay. Doobies are usually the result of high winds or telegraph wires. Not to be confused with a fooze (q.v.). Low collection value.

drop-height height from which dejecta is ejected. One Ruppel's Griffon Vulture splay had a recorded drop-height of seven miles.

dual splay two dejecta from two different birds of the same species, forming splays adjacent to each other at the same time. High collection value. (Triple splays are very rare). See also horlop.

envelope exterior container of splay containing uric acid. Usually white.

exoskeletal bony or leathery external structure e.g. insect wing casings, etc.

flarks (also skrits or skrittles, UK). Sharp gritty particles sometimes found in the nucleus of a splay, which may scratch the windscreen if dragged across it by the wiper blades.

fillmilner windscreen almost completely covered with splay matter. The result usually indicates an excellent days collection or one cormorant.

fooze splay completely disfigured by impact with windscreen. Usually due to excessive vehicle speed, high winds, or poor splay consistency. No collection value.

garl unique tangy smell produced by the rapid drying of a splay on a hot bonnet or hood. The presence of a garl is a sure sign that drying is too rapid and will result in an overly brittle specimen.

goony dried nucleus representing the only visible remains of a splay, usually resulting from the white envelope having been washed away by rain. Goonies are collectible and often mounted with pins on heavy card.

horlop splay made up of several droppings from different birds. On many occasions a perfectly good splay may become a horlop when partially or totally covered by another. Horlops have little ornithological collection value but are of increasing artistic interest, due to their exciting blend of colours and textures.

insectivorous of insects.

koote splay that restricts vision and needs to be removed before driving.

lobe pendulous extension of splay wall.

NODS National Ornithological Dejecta Society.

nucleus solid core of splay containing faecal material.

ornithology study of birds.

pav semi-solid, mainly envelopic splay that dries rapidly with a pointy meringue-like skak (q.v.).

schplerter large splay with multiple or detatched lobes.

schplutz variable sized splay with extended lobes.

skak crust forming over the top of a partially dry splay. Attempts to remove a splay from its original surface usually result in a bogor (q.v.) unless a skak has formed over the entire surface.

sklidder dejecta containing a large solid object, such as a berry stone, that skips across the windscreen leaving several splays in a straight line.

sklop small splay. See 'Splay Topography'.

splay avian dejecta containing both faecal and urate portions, formed in a spread out manner, after ejection from a height onto a hard surface. Also known as a 'spread' in Ireland, a 'whitey' in Australia, and a 'bolger'- in New Zealand. Also, v. to splay on, ie, to eject dejecta that forms a splay.

splayman person who collects and studies splays.

splerd large splay, mostly envelopic.

sploober flexible plastic tube used to suck up a wet splay and transfer it to another surface.

splood splay of variable size with a single extended lobe.

SDT Splay Drying Time.

Bibliography

BIGGS, I.T. 1987. *Identifying and Removing Splays from Solar Panels and Umbrellas.* Journal of the French Avian Dejecta Society, Vol.1, No.2.

BENTON, H.,and ROSS, R. 1990. *Happy Days with Jay Splays. A Practical Guide for Pre-schoolers.* Tricycle Press, London.

CRICHTON, A. 1990. *The Chinese Hat Method of Splay Collection.* Journal of the Lyon Avian Dejecta Society. Vol.2, No.1.

DARWIN, C. 1869. *On the Origin of Faeces.* Unpublished Manuscript and Public Lecture, Albert Hall, London.

GARRICK, R.,and PYE, W. 1991. *The Effects of Low Temperature on Splay Viscosity and Drying Time.* Journal of The Canadian Avian Dejecta League. Vol.1, No.2.

HYDE, N.O. 1990. *Creative Embellishment in the Fossil Splays of Archaeopteryx and the Pterosaurs.* Ph.D.diss., Victoria Univ., Wellington, N.Z.

McMAHON, G. 1971. *How to Read a Whitey.* Newmarlick Press, Darwin.

MALANE, D. 1989. *The Splay and Abstract Expressionism.* Ph.D.diss., Wedde Univ.Col., Toronto.

PETTIGREW, J.P. 1976. *Winter Splays. A Skier's Goggle Guide.* Fairview Press, Birmingham.

PRIOR, P. 1986. *Hygroscopicity as a Factor in the Formation of Structural Defects in Avian Dejecta.* Am. Nat. 123: 967-991.

ROSE, C.N. 1991. *Proceedings of the Second International Workshop on the Creation of Artificial Splays.* University of Tokyo Press, Tokyo.

SAINSBURY, M. 1984. *Fifty Favorite Frugivore Splays.* Scatta Press, Dublin.

SCOTT, T. 1990. *The Use of Avian Excremental Material in Tibetan Divination Ritual.* Smithsonian Institute, Washington DC.

UNWIN, M. 1989. *Splay Money. 101 Creative Ways to Exhibit and Market Ornithological Dejecta in America.* Fox Books, New York.

WHERRY, A. 1985. *Making Big Spreads. Preparing, Photographing and Blowing Up Splays in Ireland.* Bloom Books, Feakle.

WILSON, Q. 1987. *Ornithological Dejecta. Its Automorphic Significance in the Green Movement.* Encyclopedia of American Art, Simon and Putnam, New York.